Ken Saab

The Master Plan For Success

**Forewords by:
Jim Agard & Wes Street**

© Copyright 2017 - Ken Gaub

All rights reserved. This book is protected under the copyright laws of the United States of America. This book may not be copied or reprinted for commercial gain or profit. The use of short quotations or occasional page copying for personal or group study is permitted and encouraged. Permission will be granted upon request. Unless otherwise identified, Scripture quotations are from the King James Version of the Bible. Scripture quotations marked NIV are from the New International Version. Please note that the publishing style capitalizes certain pronouns in Scripture that refer to the Father, Son, and Holy Spirit, and may differ from some Bible publishers style.

Take note that the name satan and related names are not capitalized. We choose not to acknowledge him, even to the point of violating grammatical rules.

Note: The author's use of any individual's quote does not imply that the author endorses that individual's ministry or views.

"For where your treasure is, there will your heart be also." Matthew 6:21

Printed in the U.S.A.

This book and all other materials by
Ken Gaub Ministries
are available on our website at:
www.kengaub.com
509-575-1965
800-KEN-GAUB

Dedication To:

To Barbara, my wife of over 63 years. Her inspiration has always lifted me.

To Nathan, our son, for his help with this book and also our world-wide radio ministry. He has worked many hours. Also, to his wife Doris who lets us take his time.

To Becki, our daughter, whose hours of help on this book made it possible. She has worked as manager for Ken Gaub Ministries for approximately 40 years and has been involved with the ministry most of her life. We could never repay her.

To Debra Homan and my brother, Mike Gaub, who proofread this manuscript.

To my staff, board members, and Gideon Family who helped me to never give up.

To Wes Street, and his wife Jodi who have been great friends to me and this ministry. They have encouraged me, always supported, and it has been all done for "SOULS".

Forewords

Ken and I have been friends for over 35 years. We have traveled the world together with many trips to Israel. Years ago our business sponsored Ken and his band, Illustrator, to travel all over Israel for 5 weeks to perform for the Israeli army troops. Ken has always believed for miracles and continues to do what God the father in heaven instructed him to do: To share the good news that the Lord is alive and well and lives within us. Ken shares the Lord's guidelines for *The Master Plan for Success*. This is another must read for everyone.

Jim Agard
Business Owner
Fort Mill, SC

The greatest attribute we have as a human species is the ability to have a relationship with a living God. Only God and I knew I was physically dying many years ago. An evangelist on a television program offered a solution to my situation by introducing me to someone who could change any condition, if only I would believe that it could. I believed and this simple act saved my life both spiritually and physically.

I asked Dad (God, I call him Dad) to help me understand more about salvation and my role in this great act that saved me. Just a few months later Dad introduced me to Ken Gaub and his ministry.

I was talking to Dad about how thankful I was for all the things he has done and will do for me. That still small voice said, "Souls, Son. Souls". When I sit down with my CPA they ask me how can I afford to give so much. My reply is "How can I afford not to?" I then tell them that I believe Jesus is coming soon and in my lifetime, and that I will personally see this happen with my natural eyes when He returns. One of my CPAs ask "Doesn't the Bible say, "no one will know the hour?" Very true I reply, but you do not need to be standing in knee deep snow to know it's wintertime".

Sometimes I just go to a quiet place and be very still and listen, with my pencil and pad.

(It helps me remember. I don't want to miss anything). I find it interesting sometimes. He has all the answers and we do all the talking. Dad then said... you have asked me in the past about MY priorities. The expansion of My Kingdom and the souls in that Kingdom are my priorities. When you give, put these words on your checks," for the expansion of the Kingdom or Souls", to keep it ever before your face and I will multiply it accordingly. This book *"The Master Plan for Success"* will bless your future.

Wesley Street
CEO, Cornerstone Clinic Ltd.
Machesney Park, IL

Endorsements

Ken Gaub is one of the greatest soul winners I know today. Every year he comes to Word of Life International church and encourages our people to think positive and believe God for the best in their lives. Ken is always a pastor's best friend and will always encourage your people to support you, their church, and family. His books are always filled with encouraging material that will inspire you to be your best for God. As someone has said, "life is like an unsharpened pencil, without God, it has no point.

Pastor D. Wendel Cover
Word of life International Church
Springfield, Virginia

Ken Gaub has been a constant source of encouragement and support for me for over 30 years. His positive attitude and generosity is infectious. You will benefit by his insight into the *Master Plan* God has for each of us. It will give you hope, a smile, and a spring in your step knowing that God has marked you for great things in His Kingdom.

Pastor Jerry Beebe
First Assembly of God
Wenatchee, Washington

Ken Gaub was formed with an insight of the real commission. He has been one of the greatest soul winners with an insight of the *Masters Plan* to even grow a great church. He teaches how to become a soul winner which is the great commission that Jesus left for the church. He encourages everyone to become a winner in life and remember the plan with a goal in mind. He will teach you if you fail to plan, you plan to fail. You'll love this new book of Ken's.

Rev. Bill Heaston
Bill Heaston Ministries
Oviedo, Florida

God has a *Masters Plan* for each of our lives, plans to prosper us and not to harm us, plans to give us hope and a future. Our thinking can be a roadblock to this plan. Ken Gaub reveals how we can raise the level of our thinking. Ken has always been a big thinker and, as a result, has accomplished great feats for God. Let Ken help unlock your thinking so you can be all God wants you to be.

Pastor Terry L. Howell
Living Water Fellowship
Kissimmee, FL

Ken Gaub makes you laugh out loud as he directs you toward the life you were intended to live. His stories and life experiences make him a perfect vehicle to open God's Word to the revelation that helps you be a success at home, at work, in your community, and in your church. This really is <u>The Master Plan For Success</u>!

Pastor Dave Edler
Yakima Foursquare Church
Foursquare Assoc. Supervisor NW District
Former Mayor of Yakima
Played with the Mariners 6 years
Yakima, Washington

I have known Ken Gaub since 1993. I have seen his heart on many issues; helping people to know and understand faith in Christ, seems to be built into his DNA. Ken's whole life is a story of faith. His trust in God has been an encouragement in my life. I am sure this book will be a timely blessing in your life.

Pastor Ron Colemen
Grace Church Ministries
Chester, IL

Ken Gaub's Book, <u>The Master Plan for Success</u> is sure to be a must read! Success is determined by what you do in the temporal realm effects the eternal realm! Ken's life and legacy is one of daily making a difference in the lives of people everywhere. Ken Gaub has truly exemplified success at home and in ministry. This book will change your life!

Dr. Dana Gammill
Cathedral of Life
Canton, Ohio

I have watched Ken Gaub since he was in his early twenties. I saw him grow as a minister and I saw him go through many seasons in his life. I also watched him raise a family. I watched that up close because I'm his oldest son.

As I look back I realize that throughout my life, ministry, and business I have been profoundly affected by watching him. I always saw a man driven to see people find a better life through the message of the gospel of Jesus, a man that wanted to do everything he could do to see lives changed. But, as father, he always wanted to be sure that my life took the right path.

Ken Gaub is a man of God. I think this is his best book, but his best work is a family that works every day to follow in his path helping others.

Nathan Gaub
Businessman
Yakima, Washington

I have know Ken Gaub for 50 years. Ken has ministered in our church every year during most of that time and has been a great blessing to all of us. He is a man of great love and integrity, as well as, a great soul winner. You will enjoy this book.

Rev. Denny Helton
Full Gospel Temple
Muncie, IN

Ken Gaub's book *The <u>Master Plan for Success</u>* is truly a blessing for anyone that needs a fresh vision as to what God has for their future. One thing that we all need to be reminded from time to time is that God has a master plan for all of us. But there are so many people that never find the *master plan* of God because they have not entrusted in God's plan for their life or they just don't take the time to search the scriptures to find out. I find that this book lays out such a clear plan that even a war faring man can read it and walk in a new dimension of the perfect will of God. It is so down to earth and clear that if we will just read it and meditate on it we will know how much God loves us and how His *master plan* for our life is no accident, but divinely ordained for our success....

Dr. George W. Walters
Faith Outreach Center
Tampa, Florida

Contents

The Six Keys to The Master Plan

Chapter 1; Develop A Great Attitude
Page 32

Chapter 2; Forgive & Forget The Past
Page 48

Chapter 3; Waiting On God's Timing
Page 70

Chapter 4; Change What You Can
Page 82

Chapter 5; Be Positive In A Negative World
Page 94

Chapter 6; Raise The Level Of Your Faith & Expectations
Page 110

Introduction

From the very beginning of time God always had a *Master Plan* for everything He did. Things did not just happen. He planned everything he did. In creation, He had a *Master Plan* and it's spelled out in Genesis 1. He had a *Master Plan* when He created man and woman. God invented marriage so they could multiply and replenish the earth. The Old Testament stories are full of God's *Master Plan* for people. Some obeyed God and great things happened. Others disobeyed and paid a great price for it.

> "And God saw every thing that he had made, and, behold, it was very good… "
> Genesis 1:31

Read about Moses, Abraham, Isaac, Elisha and many others. There was always a *Master Plan* for their lives. It's so exciting to read these stories. I don't know if they realized it or not, but God has a *Master Plan* for each life, just like He does for us today.

> For God so loved the world, that he gave his only begotten Son, that whosoever believeth in him should not perish, but have everlasting life.
> John 3:16

In the New Testament there are many more *Master Plan* stories. John 3:16 shows God's *Master Plan* to save us. When Jesus was born in Bethlehem over 2,000 years ago, there was no back-up plan. Jesus would be born of a virgin, live a sinless life, die on the cross for us, be buried, rise from the grave and ascend back to heaven to prepare a place for us. It is so exciting, so wonderful, so uplifting. We should be thrilled just thinking about God's *Master Plan*. I trust that this book helps you see that God already has a *Master Plan* for your life.

The Master Plan

How thankful we need to be for God's blessings on our lives. I do not just count my blessings, I make my blessings count. Think about God's *Master Plan* for you. God wants you to go beyond where you have ever been in your life. He wants you to overcome the negative obstacles of life that everyone faces. He wants you to make possible the impossible that keep you from succeeding. Remember everything is impossible until it isn't. He wants you to break down barriers and reach success in every avenue of your life; spiritual, physical, emotional and financial, that you have always dreamed about. The battle may not be your choice, but the outcome of the battle is your choice.

> A big success is achieved by
> the series of small successes.
> Jim Agard

Robert Schuller said "Tough times never last, but tough people do". So remember, if your tough, the outcome of the battles that life puts you through is your choice. Someone said "Life isn't always about waiting for the storms of life to pass, but it's about learning to dance in the rain".

> [6] Wherein ye greatly rejoice, though now for a season, if need be, ye are in heaviness through manifold temptations: [7] That the trial of your faith, being much more precious than of gold that perisheth, though it be tried with fire, might be found unto praise and honour and glory at the appearing of Jesus Christ: [8] Whom having not seen, ye love; in whom, though now ye see him not, yet believing, ye rejoice with joy unspeakable and full of glory: [9] Receiving the end of your faith, even the salvation of your souls.
> 1 Peter 1:6-9

There are plenty of difficult obstacles in your path everyday, don't allow yourself to become one of those obstacles.

In this epistle, Peter is writing to Christians

that are spread throughout Asia Minor, which is modern-day Turkey. They had been scattered because of the persecution coming from Rome. These believers were being persecuted for following Christ. They were being persecuted for being different. He writes to encourage them. Here again listen to what he says in 1 Peter 1:6 In this you *greatly rejoice*, though now for a little while you may have had to *suffer grief* in all kinds of trials.

Peter says it is possible for these believers to have both great joy and grief in the midst of their trials. *This verse can also be translated as a command "rejoice in this".* The believers were suffering in all kinds of trials. The word *kinds* can be translated "various or multicolored." Some had, no doubt, lost their land, their loved ones and their careers, and yet Peter says they can still have great joy in the midst of these multicolored trials.

There have been a lot of people that I have met during my life. Some people will walk in and out of your life during a lifetime. But, some people will leave footprints of love on your heart. I am fortunate to have many great friends that stand by me no matter what we are going through. Their footprints of love are on my heart, my life, and my ministry.

God already had a *Master Plan* to bless

your life even before you were born. Do not be hijacked by negative people or negative situations. Believe that God has some good things for you in your future. You have to get ready to receive them. Matthew 6:33 is my favorite verse.

> But seek ye first the kingdom of God, and his righteousness; and all these things shall be added unto you.
> Matthew 6:33

God doesn't just want a share of your life. He wants all, 100%, 24/7, 365 days every year of your life.

> The inner you is reflected by the outer you!
> Jim Agard

I am using a King James Version of the Bible, in this book. (You do not need a King James Version of the Bible to go to heaven, but when you get there, one will be issued to you).

> "Before I formed thee in the belly", I knew thee; and before thou camest forth out of the womb I sanctified thee, and I ordained thee a prophet unto the nations. "
> Jeremiah 1:5

In Jeremiah 1:5, the Bible says "Before I formed thee in the belly", (before the sperm hit the egg in your mother's womb)..... I love that verse. It shows us that God had a *Master Plan* for us, no matter who we are or what we face, what color our skin is, what nationality we are, what country we live in or what language we speak. The devil knows this and will always try to mess it up. He will even put people or situations in your life to help mess it up. Look at how the enemy tried to mess up Adam and Eve by telling Eve, "First you will die if you eat it. Your eyes will be opened and you will be like God." She disobeyed. On the other hand, God will also bring people into your life to bless, encourage and help God's plan to work for you. Christ's victory is our victory. His triumph is our triumph.

> [1] Now the serpent was more subtil than any beast of the field which the LORD God had made. And he said unto the woman, Yea, hath God said, Ye shall not eat of every tree of the garden? [2] And the woman said unto the serpent, We may eat of the fruit of the trees of the garden: [3] But of the fruit of the tree which is in the midst of the garden, God hath said, Ye shall not eat of it, neither shall ye touch it, lest ye die. [4] And the serpent said unto the woman, Ye shall not surely die:
> Genesis 3:1-4

In Jeremiah the Bible talks about plans that God has to give you hope in the future. He has thoughts of peace for you, not of evil and wants you to always end up victorious. This is a wonderful *Master Plan*.

> "For I know the thoughts that I think toward you, saith the Lord, thoughts of peace, and not of evil, to give you an expected end."
> Jeremiah 29:11

Look at how satan messed up David in 2nd Samuel 11. David was a God-fearing man, but satan tempted him and he sinned and then had Bathsheba's husband killed in battle. This was murder.

> [2] And it came to pass in an evening tide, that David arose from off his bed, and walked upon the roof of the king's house: and from the roof he saw a woman washing herself; and the woman was very beautiful to look upon.....
> [27] And when the mourning was past, David sent and fetched her to his house, and she became his wife, and bare him a son. But the thing that David had done displeased the Lord.
> 2 Samuel 11:2 & 27

For real success in our lives, I believe that every person has a God given *Master Plan* for their life. When I think about God putting a *Master Plan* together before we were ever created in our mother's belly, I think "Wow! Is that exciting or what?" God is always on time, He knows in advance about you. I love the song, "When He Was On The Cross, I Was On His Mind". That was about 2,000 years before we were born. God has always had this *Master Plan* for your life.

I believe that there are good days ahead. Do you believe that? Do you want to see the impossible made possible. Do you want to win others to Christ? Do you want to climb over every mountain of impossibility that you face? Do you want to believe for miracles in your life and to break down the negative barriers and reach success in every avenue of your life spiritually, physically, financially, and emotionally? God has a *Master Plan* for your life, to help you have the answers and miracles you need.

> Speak what you want; not what you don't want!
> Jim Agard

Hang out with positive people, otherwise Negative people will:

Tear you down	Steal your dreams
Poison your mind	Paralyze your thinking
Hijack your future	Kill your goals

Back in the 70's Dexter Yeager's book, *Don't Let Anybody Steal Your Dreams*, stated be around people who constantly build you up and share your aspirations. They are the ones to which you like to cling too.

We all face situations in life, but you have more potential than you can ever fully develop in your lifetime. You need to develop the powers He has given you. Remember nothing is based on luck. I don't believe in luck good or bad. You say, "What about Friday the 13th?" I say that is just the day before Saturday the 14th. However, I do believe in God's divine blessings on my life. Refuse to cave in during tough times.

Take inventory of your life. There is someone (God) who is bigger than you. He can help you succeed and can save your future. Don't curse the darkness, light a candle. Your future is bright and the God who created you is on your side. Today society is cutting down their goals, fearing failure, limitations etc. They don't exercise or diet as it takes too long to get results. They don't work at reaching their goals as it requires too many nights and their days are always full. You must commit to advancing and working toward your goals to have the freedom you want and deserve.

God's *Master Plan* for you is...
To overcome obstacles.
To control circumstances.
To rise above negativism.
To be victorious.
To win battles.
To be successful in every phase of your life.

    Negative and wrong thinking will never produce positive and right results.

    If your mind dwells on disbeliefs it will attract reasons to support that disbelief. Don't let this happen.

    Read through this book, make notes on what your going to do, then do it! Now let's get into chapter one.

The road to success
doesn't always go in a straight line.
Sometimes there are detours.

Chapter 1
Develop A Great Attitude

Before we discuss the need for a great attitude, lets talk more about how your priorities determine your progress. Attitude does matter. God wants you to be the winner He created you to be.

The dictionary defines attitude as: *a settled way of thinking or feeling about someone or something, typically one that is reflected in a person's behavior.* "She took a tough attitude toward other people's indulgences".

You choose your attitude and it will define you. Attitude is about perspective. Life is all about perspective. The sinking of the Titanic was a miracle for the lobsters in the ship's kitchen. So make a choice that will define your plan in a positive direction.

It seems to me that everybody in life has some kind of *Master Plan*. In America there is a very similar layout in each Wal-Mart store. They are all basically built with the same layout. They may have something different in a store, but most Wal-Marts have a *Master Plan*. They build all of them according to that. Isn't it amazing?

Once in a while, you'll see on TV a car crashed because it had no driver. The person had died at the wheel. There are some people whose life has "no driver". A good and positive attitude will always find a way to achieve the impossible. God gives us the power to change our attitude if bad and doesn't follow God's word. A positive attitude doesn't refuse to recognize problems but it will focus on finding the answers for the problems that it faces in life. We should have the mind of Christ. This will help our attitude.

> "Let this mind be in you, which was also in Christ Jesus".
> Philippians 2:5,

If you have the mind of Christ, it will help you to have a better attitude defeating satan and his hold on your life.

> "Rejoice in the Lord always: and again I say, Rejoice". Let your moderation be known unto all men. The Lord is at hand. Be careful for nothing; but in every thing by prayer and supplication with thanksgiving let your requests be made known unto God. And the peace of God, which passeth all understanding, shall keep your hearts and minds through Christ Jesus".
> Philippians 4:4-7

God's word talks a lot about our minds. Philippians says "Rejoice in the Lord always"... He wants to guard our minds as your mind will affect your attitude. If your mind is not guarded by Jesus, your attitude will never be good. Paul said to "Gird up the loins of your mind", (1 Peter 1:13). Your mind will wander into areas you should not be in, so let Christ put a guard on your mind.

> Wherefore gird up the loins of your mind, be sober, and hope to the end for the grace that is to be brought unto you at the revelation of Jesus Christ;
> 1 Peter 1:13

Everybody has got some kind of *Master Plan*. If you go in a Subway shop to get a sandwich, they have no waitresses, no waiters. They have their own *Master Plan*. The first thing they ask is "What kind of bread do you want?" "Do you want a 6 inch or 12 inch bread"? Then you go through and pick out the rest of the stuff you want on your sandwich. That is the *Master Plan* for them.

If you go into a McDonald's, they have a *Master Plan.* It is not posted on the wall, nobody tells you that, but what you do is get in line behind the person in front of you. You do not say, "Get out of my way, I'm in a hurry!" You do not do that. They know you understand their *Master Plan* to get in line and everybody knows that is the way it works at McDonald's.

But, you go to Wendy's, and they have their own *Master Plan*. They do not trust you to get in a line. They have ropes set up so that you will stay lined up. That is the *Master Plan* for Wendy's. It works for them.

Everybody has some kind of *Master Plan.* Now those of you who are married, you may not understand it, as the man of the house, but your wife has a *Master Plan.* Every woman has some kind of a *Master Plan.* My wife said to me one day "Let's go downtown and go looking." (Nobody goes "looking", they go "shopping"). I said "Okay, I've got time, I'll go with you. We will leave the credit cards, the money and the checkbook at home since we are just "looking." And she said to me, "Well, take a credit card just in case!" See, that is part of the wife's *Master Plan* that men do not understand. So, we got in the car and she said, "Turn here" and "Go here" and "Go there." (That is why I do not have a GPS, I married one!) So we get to the store and she jumped out, and I followed her into the store. She went down this aisle and then down that aisle and there was some kind of *Master Plan* going on that I knew nothing about. We got to a table and she said, "Isn't this a beautiful table?" I said, "It looks good here, I trust people that visit this store enjoy looking at this beautiful table." She said, "We need this table." (Good thing I brought a credit card!) See, that was part of the *Master Plan* that I did not know about. We bought the table.

Now, if you have grandchildren, your grandkids have a *Master Plan*. When my grandkids were little, they would come to our house and would eat everything. They would start cooking and doing stuff and I would say "Don't you guys have food at your house?" They would say "Yes, but that was ten minutes ago and we are hungry again." They always had some kind of *Master Plan* going on. It was called "eat food."

One day I said to my two grandsons Josh & Jourdan, "We are going to pull some weeds." I live out in the country on 10 acres and I said, "We are going to pull some weeds and you are not going to get paid." That was my *Master Plan*. I said, "We are not paying you because you eat all of our food most of the time anyway. We want you to pull the weeds because you love us. We are your grandparents and you do not have to always be paid for helping us." They said, "Okay!" So, they went out and I was helping them and I heard Jourdan say to Josh, "Man, it is hot out here! I feel dizzy" He said, "You know I need a Pepsi, but since we are not getting paid for this, we have no money, because we are doing this because we love them." I could hear this whole conversation. They had a *Master Plan* going on. He said to his brother, "Now, if I faint and fall down, you call the ambulance and take me to the hospital. Tell them that Grandpa is not paying us today so there is no money and this all happened because I did not get a Pepsi. We are pulling weeds because we love them." So, I took them inside the house and got both of them a Pepsi. You see, they had a *Master Plan*.

Everybody has some kind of a *Master Plan* going on. One little kid said to his grandpa, "Grandpa! Make a sound like a frog!" Grandpa said, "I do not want to make a sound like a frog". The kid said "Please Grandpa! Make a sound like a frog!" Grandpa finally said, "Why do you want me to make a sound like a frog?" The kid said, "Because Grandma said that when you croak, we are going to Disneyland!" You see, everybody has some kind of a *Master Plan*.

Now there are <u>six keys</u> I want to give you about God's *Master Plan* in your life. If God has a *Master Plan*, and it is possible for you to mess it up with disobedience, it must also be possible for you to help encourage that *Master Plan* to work if you follow what God wants to do in your life. The pieces of the puzzle will fit together.

I get excited about it. Don't you? God has a *Master Plan* for your life. Remember, God is supply oriented not just need oriented.

When my grandkids were small and stayed at our house often, I was supply oriented and not need oriented. One time about 3 in the morning, my daughter Becki and her husband Santiago, their children, Austin and Brittney, were staying with us. They came upstairs in our room and woke us up. I turned on the light and Brittney was standing with her arm around Austin. Austin's pajamas were gone. We didn't put him to bed that way. He was just in a pair of shorts. He had an accident, tried to flush his pajamas down the toilet and that was the reason we had a flood downstairs, which I don't want to discuss now. I said to them, "What do you want?" They said, "Corn flakes". They said, "Yes". I jumped out of bed and headed to the kitchen. I said, "Lets put ice cream on the corn flakes, they said, "yes," and we had a party, because I was supply oriented not need oriented. God will not do it exactly like that, but He is supply oriented not just need oriented.

> *One of the greatest blessings in life is keeping a positive attitude when others around you are always negative.*

I trust this book will help you to understand the need of a right strategy, in order to leave the past and step into the future and have God's *Master Plan* work in your life. God has given you power to believe Him. If you keep thinking you can't do something - you're right. If you keep thinking you can do something – you're right. If you get involved with God, He will get involved with you. You have got to know who you are. This will help you when it's time to fight for what you need. You may have to fight for the people who mean the most in your life.

Maybe fight for the job you really want. You may have to fight when people say you can't do something. You may have to fight for opportunities to open for you. You will have lived a blessed life if you fight for the things that you know are promised in the Word of God. Your greatest victories can be won on your knees. Know your battle area.

When an alligator fights a bear, usually the bear wins in the woods and the alligator wins in the water. Remember, even satan has a plan for your life. He is a deceiver, a liar, a destroyer, and one who also tempts. His strength is his ability to do this stuff. He will come as an angel of light. He is a master of deception, he is a counterfeit. Don't underestimate satan. Ephesians 6:13-17, talks about your "whole armour of God".

> "Wherefore take unto you the whole armour of God, that ye may be able to withstand in the evil day, and having done all, to stand. Stand therefore, having your loins girt about with truth, and having on the breastplate of righteousness; And your feet shod with the preparation of the gospel of peace; Above all, taking the shield of faith, wherewith ye shall be able to quench all the fiery darts of the wicked. And take the helmet of salvation, and the sword of the Spirit, which is the word of God."
> Ephesians 6:13-17

I believe the number one point is that we have got to produce some kind of a good attitude, no matter what happens to us. Believe me, you need a great attitude. Ever had a bad attitude? We have got to have a good attitude in our life, on the job, with our marriage, with our kids, and also in the church. Wherever we go, we have got to have a good attitude, if we want God's *Master Plan* to work for us. Your attitude is more important than your I.Q.

When Clair Booth Luce was the ambassador to Italy, she lived in her residence, a great villa from the 17th century. She began to notice physical deterioration. She lost energy, lost weight, and was always tired. Her physical condition worsened. She sought medical help and discovered she was suffering from arsenic poisoning. The staff was checked out and they were found trustworthy. Where was the arsenic coming from? Finally, they discovered the pretty roses painted on the celling contained arsenic lead. Fine dust fell from the painted roses. She was slowly being poisoned. Our attitude and concepts can be poisoned by the people around us. Sometimes we are unware until the damage has been done.

Faith and a good attitude are twins, one will always be found with the other.

> Faith without action is dead!
> Jim Agard

Jesus didn't teach us to deny the existence of problems. Some say if you are sick or have a disease, ignore it and some even say you don't have it. If you break your leg you can't ignore it. If it is broken, it is broken. It can be fixed or healed if you believe for it, but just to deny the problem exists is not even scriptural or sensible. Jesus knew sickness would be so real so He let them put those stripes on His back. By His stripes we are healed.

I've told millions of people there is no such thing as a hopeless situation. Some may grow hopeless about their situation.

Napoleon and Helen Keller are great illustrations. Napoleon had riches and power and glory. However, he said he had never known 6 happy days in this life. Helen Keller who was both blind and deaf, said, "I have found life so beautiful." She also said it must be sad to have good eyes that can't see. You have the power to choose the attitude you want. Why not choose to have a good attitude.

There are some times when we do not have a good attitude. It's because we have let somebody hijack our life and our good attitude. They will hijack our joy and run us down, if we allow it. There are always people that will do that. However, no one can make you a failure without your consent. You just cannot please everybody, but God has a *Master Plan* for our life and it is so good that He has got this *Master Plan* already laid out for us. He has put it all together for your life, even before you were born.

> *Choose to have a good attitude!*

Now I have a good attitude, even when I am not happy. I am not happy when I have a flat tire, but I have a good attitude because I had three tires that did not blow out. There is always something to be happy about. Positive people look for the good. Negative people always look for the bad.

When I started traveling, speaking at revivals many years ago, we did not have pictures. People did not know what we looked like until we arrived. We did not have posters, we did not have anything. We just went to the meetings and if they didn't know us they did not know what we looked like until we got there.

We were headed to a meeting when I came into St. Louis and a car pulled out from a side street and nearly hit me. So, I laid on the horn, because that is what horns are for, to honk at idiots. (You know, God gave man the ability to invent a horn. So, it is a God thing). I told my wife, I laid on the horn to let him know that what I am doing is what God wants me to do, to honk at idiots. So, I pulled up to the red light and he pulled up beside me in the other lane and looked at me and I looked at him. We did not like each other. He was an idiot. It was just one of those things. When the light turned green I took off and he took off. We stopped at the next light and looked at each other, we still didn't like each other (he was an idiot). Finally at the next light I had to turn left, so as I turned, I laid on the horn again. You know, to let him know that I am leaving now. He went straight and he laid on his horn. We were both mad! Well, I got over to the pastor's house, and I knocked on the door. Well, guess who opened the door? It was that man. I looked at him and he looked at me. We both could not believe it. Here is that man that nearly hit me. So, I finally said to him, "Well, it was your fault." He said, "Well, I shouldn't have been driving that way." I said "Yeah, I know. That is why I had to honk like that, because you were driving that way." I said, "Is the meeting over?" I thought he might cancel the meeting. He said, "Oh Ken, we both learned a great lesson about attitude." He threw his arms around me and hugged me. To this day, we still laugh about it. So, we both learned something from that. He tells the same story. Of course, he tells it a little different than I do. Anyway, that is just the way it was.

Our attitude is very important. I just said, I believe that God in His mercy does not just want a share of your life; He wants all of your life. He wants your attitude to be great. I believe sometimes God allows events, situations and circumstances to see how we are going to react. Life is about 10% of what happens to us and 90% of how we react to what happens to us. Never make a permanent decision based on a temporary situation. Your life will always rise or fall on the decisions you make everyday. The pressures of life help to shape us, just like great pressure produces diamonds from a piece of coal. We have to work on always having a great attitude.

God wants you to be a winner.

Are you a winner	Or loser
Part of the Answer	Part of the Problem
Get things done	Makes Excuses
Says lets helps	says not my Job
See Possibilities	See the impossible
Jumps the hurdles	Quits, it's too hard
Is a giver	Is a taker
Has faith	Has fear
Believes what you can't see	Believes only what is seen
Falls down, but gets up	Falls down, says somebody pushed me
Says is difficult, but possible	It may be possible, but too difficult
On the building crew	on the wrecking crew

To develop a great attitude, I need to change...

1. _____

2. _____

3. _____

4. _____

Chapter 2
Forgive and Forget the Past

First, let's look at two things. Number one, guilt. That is when we do something wrong.

Number two, bitterness. That happens when someone does something wrong against you.

When you forgive, you set two people free. yourself and the other person too. You forgive because God has forgiven you. That is called grace.

Years ago, a man stole some money from the company he worked for. He was caught and summoned to the CEO's office. With a heavy heart he went, knowing his job was probably over. The CEO asked, "Did you do this thing?"

The man said, "Yes, I did". The CEO said "If I forgave you, could I ever trust you again?" The man said "Yes, and I'll be the best employee you ever had." The CEO said, "I forgive you, but let me tell you something. Years ago at this same company I did what you did and I was forgiven, so I forgive you."

Forgiveness is the act of pardoning an offender. In the Bible, the Greek word translated "forgiveness" literally means "to let go," as when a person does not demand payment for a debt. Jesus used this comparison when he taught his followers to pray:

> And forgive us our sins; for we also forgive every one that is indebted to us.
> Luke 11:4a

Likewise, in his parable of the unmerciful slave, Jesus equated forgiveness with canceling a debt.

> [23] Therefore is the kingdom of heaven likened unto a certain king, which would take account of his servants. [24] And when he had begun to reckon, one was brought unto him, which owed him ten thousand talents. [25] But forasmuch as he had not to pay, his lord commanded him to be sold, and his wife, and children, and all that he had, and payment to be made. [26] The servant therefore fell down, and worshipped him, saying, Lord, have patience with me, and I

will pay thee all. [27] Then the lord of that servant was moved with compassion, and loosed him, and forgave him the debt. [28] But the same servant went out, and found one of his fellowservants, which owed him an hundred pence: and he laid hands on him, and took him by the throat, saying, Pay me that thou owest. [29] And his fellowservant fell down at his feet, and besought him, saying, Have patience with me, and I will pay thee all. [30] And he would not: but went and cast him into prison, till he should pay the debt. [31] So when his fellowservants saw what was done, they were very sorry, and came and told unto their lord all that was done. [32] Then his lord, after that he had called him, said unto him, O thou wicked servant, I forgave thee all that debt, because thou desiredst me: [33] Shouldest not thou also have had compassion on thy fellowservant, even as I had pity on thee? [34] And his lord was wroth, and delivered him to the tormentors, till he should pay all that was due unto him. [35] So likewise shall my heavenly Father do also unto you, if ye from your hearts forgive not every one his brother their trespasses.

Matthew 18:23-35

In verse 24, it talks about talents. This was the largest measure of money in the Roman world. When Solomon built the temple it was overlaid with 8,000 talents of gold. A man worked for 100 pence a day so 10,000 talents would take 17,000 men working 10 years. This man would never be able to pay this debt.

We forgive others when we let go of resentment and give up any claim to be compensated for the hurt or loss we have suffered. The Bible teaches that unselfish love is the basis for true forgiveness, since love does not keep account or even save all the information to show others.

> [4] Love is patient, love is kind. It does not envy, it does not boast, it is not proud. [5] It does not dishonor others, it is not self-seeking, it is not easily angered, it keeps no record of wrongs.
> 1 Corinthians 13:4-5 (NIV)

We have to forgive and forget the past. In this context, it means not to "hold it against" someone any longer. This is different than the lack of memory. This is an actual, willful choice you have to make. Forgetting is one of the toughest things to do. We really have to work on this. How many of you have had someone rip you off? Made a decision about you that had bad results. Someone lied and told something that was not true about you? Maybe sued you just for money. Somebody that treated you badly? All of that kind of bad stuff and maybe a lot of other things. The past and future don't even exist. You have to forgive and forget all of that. What does it mean to really forgive?

> "Blessed are ye, when men shall revile you, and persecute you, and shall say all manner of evil against you falsely, for my sake. Rejoice, and be exceeding glad: for great is your reward in heaven: for so persecuted they the prophets which were before you."
> Matthew 5:11-12

Wow! If you are persecuted, falsely accused, reviled, you are blessed and are to rejoice! Just be sure it was for His name's sake.

Arni Jacobson wrote a great book, *The High Cost of Resentment*. He said "resentment will destroy any container it is carried in". Unresolved resentment, unforgiveness will destroy your future. Arni states, to be angry and hurting is normal.

> Resentment will destroy
> any container it is carried in.
>
> Arni Jacobson

Peter asked Jesus how many times to forgive?

> "Lord, how oft shall my brother sin against me, and I forgive him? till seven times? Jesus saith unto him, I say not unto thee, Until seven times: but, Until seventy times seven."
> Matthew 18:21-22

Jesus gave power and authority to every believer, to forgive those who do things against us.

> "But to which of the angels said he at any time, Sit on my right hand, until I make thine enemies thy footstool?"
> Hebrews 1:13

A person who doesn't forgive those who have wronged them, will never have peace of mind or accomplish real success. Tom Watson of IBM was asked if he was going to fire an employee where a mistake cost IBM $600,000. He said "No, I just spent $600,000 training him. Why would I want someone to hire his experience? He made a mistake, but he will work and help us recover the loss".

> *We can put the enemy under our feet.*
> *You are in charge and have a God given power and the authority to win.*
> *It will kill your enemy.*
> George Waters

If you continue to think about it, talk about it, you haven't really let it go. It will wear you down if you let it. It will not be good for you in many ways, even your health. The Bible states in Matthew that this is a very serious thing. Think about it. Not forgiving someone could send you to hell. We are to pray for our enemies. Not a prayer like "God, wipe them out". If you pray that way, you haven't really forgiven them. In today's world people are encouraged not to forgive but to sue and take legal action.

> [14] For if ye forgive men their trespasses, your heavenly Father will also forgive you: [15] But if ye forgive not men their trespasses, neither will your Father forgive your trespasses.
> Matthew 6:14-15

Several years ago our youngest son, Dan, was killed in a motorcycle accident. Someone said that if Barbara and I were closer to God, then our son would not have died, as well as all kinds of other bad things. We had to forgive and forget that. We had to live above that. My wife said to me one day, "You have got to forgive those people." I said "I am working on that." It was tough for me. We have to take authority over the power of the enemy as Jesus said in John.

> Verily, verily, I say unto you, He that believeth on me, the works that I do shall he do also; and greater works than these shall he do; because I go unto my Father.
> John 14:12

You will live longer, you will feel better, your food will digest better, you will sleep better at night, and your life will be happier if you forgive and forget the past. It is just the way it should be. When you hold on to your hatred, your pain, your hurt will take a toll on your emotions and even your health. Maybe you feel the person doesn't even deserve your forgiveness. I've seen people that couldn't get a miracle until they asked someone for forgiveness.

A Korean student walked to mail a letter when he was attacked by a group of boys. Before he could be taken to a hospital, he died. The boys who killed him were identified and arrested. The family of the Korean boy was greatly impacted by the ministry of Dr. Cho who pastors the largest church in the world with approximately a million people. I love ministering there. They wrote the court and asked them to greatly decrease sentencing of the boys who killed their son. They even started a fund to help the boys when they were released from prison. Even though they hated the killing of their son, they forgave those who did it. That was real forgiveness.

> *Forgiveness is a cancelled note,*
> *torn in pieces and burned in the fire.*

The Bible says a lot about forgiveness and unforgiveness. I just mentioned the most well-known teaching on this is Jesus' parable of the unmerciful servant, in Matthew 18:21-

35. In this parable, a king forgives an enormously large debt (basically one that could never be repaid) of one of his servants. Later, however, that same servant refuses to forgive the small debt of another man. The king hears about this and rescinds his prior forgiveness. Here again is Matthew 18 I want you to really remember this story.

> [21] Then came Peter to him, and said, Lord, how oft shall my brother sin against me, and I forgive him? till seven times? [22] Jesus saith unto him, I say not unto thee, Until seven times: but, Until seventy times seven. [23] Therefore is the kingdom of heaven likened unto a certain king, which would take account of his servants. [24] And when he had begun to reckon, one was brought unto him, which owed him ten thousand talents. [25] But forasmuch as he had not to pay, his lord commanded him to be sold, and his wife, and children, and all that he had, and payment to be made. [26] The servant therefore fell down, and worshipped him, saying, Lord, have patience with me, and I will pay thee all. [27] Then the lord of that servant was moved with compassion, and loosed him, and forgave him the debt. [28] But the same servant went out, and found one of his fellowservants, which owed him an hundred pence: and he laid hands on him, and took him by the throat, saying, Pay me that thou owest. [29] And his fellowservant fell down at his feet, and besought him, saying,

> Have patience with me, and I will pay thee all. [30] And he would not: but went and cast him into prison, till he should pay the debt. [31] So when his fellowservants saw what was done, they were very sorry, and came and told unto their lord all that was done. [32] Then his lord, after that he had called him, said unto him, O thou wicked servant, I forgave thee all that debt, because thou desiredst me: [33] Shouldest not thou also have had compassion on thy fellowservant, even as I had pity on thee? [34] And his lord was wroth, and delivered him to the tormentors, till he should pay all that was due unto him.
>
> Matthew 18:21-34

Jesus concludes by saying Matthew 18:35.

> [35] So likewise shall my heavenly Father do also unto you, if ye from your hearts forgive not every one his brother their trespasses.
>
> Matthew 18:35

Other passages tell us that we will be forgiven as we forgive.

> For if ye forgive men their trespasses, your heavenly Father will also forgive you:
> Matthew 6:14

> For with what judgment ye judge, ye shall be judged: and with what measure ye mete, it shall be measured to you again.
> Matthew 7:2
>
> Judge not, and ye shall not be judged: condemn not, and ye shall not be condemned: forgive, and ye shall be forgiven:
> Luke 6:37

If you don't forgive, God said He can not forgive you. This needs to sink in so we understand how serious it is.

Do not be confused here; God's forgiveness is not based on our works. Forgiveness and salvation are founded completely in God and by what Jesus did on the cross. However, God's *Master Plan* is achieved when we understand that what God and Jesus did only works when we forgive others and demonstrate our faith and understanding of God's grace.

> [14] What doth it profit, my brethren, though a man say he hath faith, and have not works? can faith save him? [15] If a brother or sister be naked, and destitute of daily food, [16] And one of you say unto them, Depart in peace, be ye warmed and filled; notwithstanding ye give them not those things which are needful to the body; what doth it profit? [17] Even so faith, if it hath not works, is

dead, being alone. [18] Yea, a man may say, Thou hast faith, and I have works: shew me thy faith without thy works, and I will shew thee my faith by my works. [19] Thou believest that there is one God; thou doest well: the devils also believe, and tremble. [20] But wilt thou know, O vain man, that faith without works is dead? [21] Was not Abraham our father justified by works, when he had offered Isaac his son upon the altar? [22] Seest thou how faith wrought with his works and by works was faith made perfect? [23] And the scripture was fulfilled which saith, Abraham believed God, and it was imputed unto him for righteousness: and he was called the Friend of God. [24] Ye see then how that by works a man is justified, and not by faith only. [25] Likewise also was not Rahab the harlot justified by works, when she had received the messengers, and had sent them out another way? [26] For as the body without the spirit is dead, so faith without works is dead also.

James 2:14-26

Wherefore I say unto thee, Her sins, which are many, are forgiven; for she loved much: but to whom little is forgiven, the same loveth little.

Luke 7:47

We are completely unworthy, yet Jesus chose to pay the price for our sins and to give us forgiveness.

> But God commendeth his love toward us, in that, while we were yet sinners, Christ died for us.   Romans 5:8

When we really understand God's gift to us, we will pass the gift along. We have been covered by God's grace and should cover others in return. In the parable, we are appalled at the servant not forgiving a minor debt after having been forgiven his massive debt. Yet, when we are unforgiving, we act just like the servant in the parable.

> **Make no mistake about it, unforgiveness will stop all of God's plans for you.**

Remember Jacob who worked for seven years to get Rebekah and had to work an extra seven years, because he was tricked. His heart must have been full of unforgiveness.

> [16] And Laban had two daughters: the name of the elder was Leah, and the name of the younger was Rachel. [17] Leah was tender eyed; but Rachel was beautiful and well favoured. [18] And Jacob loved Rachel; and said, I will serve thee seven years for Rachel thy younger daughter…. [20] And Jacob served seven years for Rachel; and they seemed unto him but a few days, for the love he had to her…. [23] And it came

> to pass in the evening, that he took Leah his daughter, and brought her to him; and he went in unto her. ²⁵ And it came to pass, that in the morning, behold, it was Leah: and he said to Laban, What is this thou hast done unto me? did not I serve with thee for Rachel? wherefore then hast thou beguiled me?
> Genesis 29:16-18, 20, 23, 25

Then there is Joseph. He was his dad's favorite, his brothers ganged up on him and tried to kill him but sold him into slavery and then he was put in prison. They lied to his dad and said animals killed him. While he could have been bitter, he chose to keep true to God.

> ⁴ And when his brethren saw that their father loved him more than all his brethren, they hated him, and could not speak peaceably unto him..... ²⁴ And they took him, and cast him into a pit..... ³¹ And they took Joseph's coat, and killed a kid of the goats, and dipped the coat in the blood; ³² And they sent the coat of many colours, and they brought it to their father.....³⁶ And the Midianites sold him into Egypt unto Potiphar, an officer of Pharaoh's, and captain of the guard.
> Genesis 37:4, 24, 31-32, 36

However, at about 30 years old, God had something great for him, God blessed him to a new position in the king's palace. Now he rose to being a real leader, under Pharaoh. Nothing happens by chance with God.

> [21] But the Lord was with Joseph, and shewed him mercy, and gave him favour in the sight of the keeper of the prison. [4] And Joseph said unto his brethren, Come near to me, I pray you. And they came near. And he said, I am Joseph your brother, whom ye sold into Egypt. [5] Now therefore be not grieved, nor angry with yourselves, that ye sold me hither: for God did send me before you to preserve life..... [8] So now it was not you that sent me hither, but God: and he hath made me a father to Pharaoh, and lord of all his house, and a ruler throughout all the land of Egypt. [19] And Joseph said unto them, Fear not: for am I in the place of God? [20] But as for you, ye thought evil against me; but God meant it unto good, to bring to pass, as it is this day, to save much people alive.
> Genesis 39:21, 45:4,5,8 & 50:19-20

Start praising God that you have a forgiving heart. My wife and I said when we got married "As for me and my house, we will serve the Lord". That means in good times and in bad times.

> "I will bless the Lord at all times: His praise shall continually be in my month".
> Psalm 34:1

This is an important thing in our lives. The past does not represent what you're capable of achieving during your lifetime. God has a *Master Plan* for your life.

Your life moves in the direction of your most dominant thoughts. Fill your heart and mind with good thoughts, even of forgiveness, and your life will start moving in the right directions.

Michael Jordan missed 9,000 basketball shots, lost over 3,000 games and was trusted 26 times to make a shot to win and failed. But he forgot the past and became a real winner.

Babe Ruth struck out many times but went down in history as a great baseball player because he forgot the past. You'll never be the best if you keep looking for the worst. Every day, no matter what happens, forgive and forget the past.

In 1954, Roger Banister ran a 4 minute mile, which had never been done before. He had to believe he could do it and he did. Then in 1955 almost 60 people did it, and in 1956 over 300 did it.

It doesn't matter if lies are told about you or what has been brought against you. God is keeping the real records. If someone comes against you, they will reap what they sow, big time.

In 460 B.C. the king made a feast. Then the queen Vashti also made a feast and refused to go to the King's feast. The king got mad and said I'll give her crown to another. There was a Jewish girl named Esther. So he chose Esther over all of the beautiful virgins. Then he gave Esther the queen's position. Esther's life was at stake. She said, (Esther 4:16). "...If I perish, I perish". Her uncle was Mordecai, who actually raised her. Haman, Mordecai's enemy, could not or would not forgive and it cost him his life. He was hung on the gallows made for Mordechai. This is a great story about forgiveness and what happens when we don't forgive.

It's so important, everyday no matter what happens you must forgive and forget the past. Someone cost me a lot of money years ago. I co-signed a note for him with his promise to pay as agreed. He defaulted after a couple of payments and I had to repay the note. It was hard for me to forgive him, but I did. Then God blessed me in financial ways. You may have to move out of your comfort zone sometimes and forgive. It may be tough, but God will reward you.

My friend of over 50 years, Dan Wold, said

someone who owed him money went broke. Dan kept a good spirit and prospered even without the money owed to him.

How are you doing on forgiving people and forgetting the past? It's a must if God's Master Plan is going to bless you.

How to forgive someone:

1. **Remember what forgiveness involves.**
You are not condoning the wrong or acting as if it never happened—you are simply letting it go.

2. **Recognize the benefits of forgiving.**
Letting go of anger and resentment can help you to keep calm, improve your health, and increase your happiness. (Proverbs 14:30; Matthew 5:9) Even more important, forgiving others is a key to receiving God's forgiveness for your own sins.—Matthew 6:14-15.

A sound heart is the life of the flesh: but envy the rottenness of the bones.
                    Proverbs 14:30

Blessed are the peacemakers: for they shall be called the children of God.
                    Matthew 5:9

> For if ye forgive men their trespasses, your heavenly Father will also forgive you: But if ye forgive not men their trespasses, neither will your Father forgive your trespasses.
> Matthew 6:14-15

3. **Be empathetic.**
   All of us are imperfect. (James) Just as we appreciate being forgiven, we should likewise forgive the mistakes of others. (Matthew).

> For in many things we offend all. If any man offend not in word, the same is a perfect man, and able also to bridle the whole body.
> James 3:2
>
> Therefore all things whatsoever ye would that men should do to you, do ye even so to them: for this is the law and the prophets.
> Matthew 7:12

4. **Be reasonable.**
   When we have a minor cause for complaint, we can apply the Bible's counsel: "Continue putting up with one another." (Colossians).

> Forbearing one another, and forgiving one another, if any man have a quarrel against any: even as Christ forgave you, so also do ye.
> Colossians 3:13

5. **Act quickly.**
   Work to forgive as soon as you can rather than letting your anger fester. (Ephesians).

> [26] Be ye angry, and sin not: let not the sun go down upon your wrath: [27] Neither give place to the devil.
> Ephesians 4:26-27

To forgive and forget the past, I need to change...

1. _____

2. _____

3. _____

4. _____

Chapter 3
Waiting on God's Timing

Remember part of God's *Master Plan* is the timing. When a builder builds a house he has a plan. Part of that plan is the timing. He does not have the people come to install the lights before the walls are up. Everything has an order. Each phase of the plan prepares the house for the next. The builder knows the order that the plan must have to succeed.

God knows his plan for you and every phase that must happen. Remember the last thing got you ready for the next thing.

Sometimes being patient is very

hard. When we're bringing our needs to God again and again, we get very tired of waiting. It soon begins to feel like our prayers are not being heard. What we want to do is to take control and just "do the best we can;" it is our reaction to the silence. We know Galatians 5 lists patience as a fruit of the Holy Spirit yet we confess our desire to rule our own lives. We ask the Spirit to fill us, empowering and directing us even as we continue to wait on God.

This doesn't mean circumstances change. Your only child is sick in the hospital, the struggle of your marriage continues to grow, or the hope you've held on to for years is fading. You have prayed and believed that what you are facing would be resolved by now, but the problem persists. It's easy to feel your patience running out. On these days, let these reminders on the nature of patience be an encouragement to you as you continue to wait.

When my younger son was killed in an accident, I did not understand how that could be part of any plan God had. But the Bible says it is.

> And we know that all things work together for

> good to them that love God, to them who are the called according to his purpose.
> Romans 8:28

It did not say all things were good... but work together for good.

Waiting is a common experience. All your brothers and sisters in faith, as well as all of creation know what it is like to wait on God.

> [22] For we know that the whole creation groaneth and travaileth in pain together until now. [23] And not only they, but ourselves also, which have the firstfruits of the Spirit, even we ourselves groan within ourselves, waiting for the adoption, to wit, the redemption of our body. [24] For we are saved by hope: but hope that is seen is not hope: for what a man seeth, why doth he yet hope for? [25] But if we hope for that we see not, then do we with patience wait for it.
> Romans 8:22-25

Consider those who have waited before you: Job, David, lots of prophets all had to learn to wait. The Bible has a lot to tell us about a need for patience and those who have excelled at it.

> Be patient therefore, brethren, unto the coming of the Lord. Behold, the husbandman waiteth for the precious fruit of the earth, and hath long patience for it, until he receive the early and latter rain.
> James 5:7
> [10] That ye might walk worthy of the Lord unto all pleasing, being fruitful in every good work, and increasing in the knowledge of God; [11] Strengthened with all might, according to his glorious power, unto all patience and longsuffering with joyfulness; [12] Giving thanks unto the Father, which hath made us meet to be partakers of the inheritance of the saints in light:
> Colossians 1:10-12
>
> I waited patiently for the Lord; and he inclined unto me, and heard my cry.
> Psalm 40:1
>
> Here is the patience of the saints: here are they that keep the commandments of God, and the faith of Jesus.
> Revelation 14:12

These are just a few examples. Many more exist.

One Bible dictionary defines patience as "God-given restraint in the face of opposition or oppression."

Patience is only needed when there is a reason to *not* wait. It is only necessary in the face of opposition. This is why seeking patience is in many senses a battle. The promise we can lean on here is that patience is a God-given thing. The Lord is the one who provides us with spiritual armor to go into battle. We think of patience as endurance, waiting for the trial to pass, this is just not true. We are not exercising restraint on our own strength. In truth, our only responsibility is to trust that God will provide the strength to hold on, and then act accordingly to our faith in that promise.

How is this strength given to us? We receive this strength by being filled with God's Spirit. As Christians, we know that the ultimate source of patience lives within us. Our role is to trust that God knows what he is doing and that his timing is perfect.

I remember seeing a businessman, Donald Trump, on TV in an interview in 2010. He said I have no desire to run for the President of the United States of America. However, he said, I will wait and see where we are headed. If it looks like America is going down the wrong road, then I may run for the presidency and if I do run, I will expect to win. I told my wife he speaks like a president. When I saw him in the running against about 16 others, I said, He will be president if that is what God's *Master Plan* is. I may not agree with all he says or does, but I believe God is in control and we should back him and pray for him to succeed.

The experience of waiting on God reminds us that the reality of God's *Master Plan* is beyond our understanding. We must trust that the next step in the plan will take us into a place that we will see the previous step made us ready for the next.

> God always prepares us for where He is going to take us.
> Jerry Beebe

In the Old Testament there was a prophet named Habakkuk. He saw great issues in the nation and he went to God and complained. God told him that a time of justice was coming. Habakkuk told the nation and then it did not happen. He looked like he was just a crazy guy making the whole thing up.

He went to God and asked if God forgot what he told him. God's answer was one of the best verses in the Bible.

> ² And the LORD answered me, and said, Write the vision, and make it plain upon tables, that he may run that readeth it. ³ For the vision is yet for an appointed time, but at the end it shall speak, and not lie: though it tarry, wait for it; because it will surely come, it will not tarry. ⁴ Behold, his soul which is lifted up is not upright in him: but the just shall live by his faith.
> Habakkuk 2:2-4

God was telling him it will happen and when it does it will not be one day overdue. Patience is also supposed to be a part of our everyday life.

I personally struggle with having patience. I have to really work on it. While writing this book, I wanted to have it done by the summer. We are now close to the new year and are still finishing up the last details. I told my daughter, Becki, I wanted it done before now. She smiles and said, "It will be done in God's time, not yours". God is always working on my patience.

An example from the life of Christ illustrates this. Jesus was very patient with his disciples. They were sometimes thickheaded, lazy, selfish, and slow to believe. We can see how frustrating they must have been.

In spite of Jesus' miracles and words of wisdom, they were focused upon themselves. They even wavered in their belief about who He really was. That had to be uncomfortable for Jesus. Yet we do not find him yelling at his disciples over their foolishness. He did not make fun of them when they made mistakes.

Occasionally he does remark that his disciples are slow to believe, He asks how long they will fail to have faith in him, but these are just reminders about just what was at stake for them. These were fitting and useful rebukes, not petty venting.

His refusal to complain also involves humility, the conscious decision to lower himself by not exercising his right to judge and dismiss his friends because of their faults. We might even say this is a form of mercy.

What is our role in this battle? God allows us to access patience, but it is our choice to accept it and act in willful obedience. Adam and Eve were given complete free will. They were given many things in the garden so they wouldn't need to eat the forbidden fruit. But, they chose to disobey God's command. When we use God-given patience to wait on His will and timing, we renounce their sinful act and move in obedience towards God.

There is purpose in the process. Take a look at this scripture.

> Looking unto Jesus the author and finisher of our faith; who for the joy that was set before him endured the cross, despising the shame, and is set down at the right hand of the throne of God.
> Hebrews 12:2

"The Finisher of our faith". It requires faith to have patience. Jesus brings faith in your life and that equals patience.

Waiting on God forces us to look to Him for the next step in His plan for us. It means we rely on Christ as the source of our faith and the assurance of our salvation. Trials cause us to grow by increasing our knowledge of God and relying on Him more intentionally. As James tells us, it is here that a mature and complete faith is grown.

> [2] My brethren, count it all joy when ye fall into divers temptations; [3] Knowing this, that the trying of your faith worketh patience. [4] But let patience have her perfect work, that ye may be perfect and entire, wanting nothing.
> James 1:2-4

Standing patiently when we wait on the Lord does not mean being stuck at a standstill. Consider Ephesians which instructs us to put on the full armor of God, so that when the day of evil comes, you may be able to stand your ground, and after you have done everything, to stand. Then stand firm.

> Wherefore take unto you the whole armour of God, that ye may be able to withstand in the evil day, and having done all, to stand.
> Ephesians 6:13

To hold ground by remaining obedient to the Lord while waiting is not passive. Note that the word **stand** is repeated two times. Patience is an act of the will to claim ground for the Kingdom of God, and is rewarded richly by Him. Revelation tells us of God's care for those who persevere through the battle.

> [10] Because thou hast kept the word of my patience, I also will keep thee from the hour of temptation, which shall come upon all the world, to try them that dwell upon the earth. [11] Behold, I come quickly: hold that fast which thou hast, that no man take thy crown.
> Revelation 3:10-11

Part of His *Master Plan* for success in our lives is growing in strength. Success is in part the strength to handle anything and come out on the other side with victory.

Why do we feel we lack patience to wait on God? Or maybe we struggle to continue to care for those that may be hard to love. Remember you do have all the patience you need. You can trust God to give you the strength to live above our circumstances and instead use the time of waiting to grow in understanding of His *Master Plan* for your life.

To wait on God's timing, I need to change...

1._____

2._____

3._____

4._____

Chapter 4
Change What You Can

I think it is really important to change what we can in our life. There is nothing people hate more than **change.** I dislike it myself. Years ago I handed in my first book and the publisher didn't change one word. The word they didn't change was on page 73.

We hate the change because we are comfortable with the way things are and we fear change will be less comfortable.

If we want to grow in God's plan we will have to want to change some things in our lives. Assassinate, bury and burn all negatives that hinder us from getting answers.

You cannot change everything. You cannot change your birthday. I just tell people that I am now about thirty-nine plus shipping and handling. There is nothing I can do about it.

You cannot change what people say about you or what people think about you. They may even criticize you. You cannot even change the decisions made by others about you. They may know no real facts, but remember God is keeping the real records. So lies or whatever will cost them, not you. You cannot change that. Again, there is nothing you can do about it. So don't waste your time trying. Live a happy life and change what you can.

You cannot change the death of a friend or a relative. (If I could and had the money, I would have paid a million dollars for my son, Dan, not to have died, but I couldn't change that). There was absolutely nothing I could do about the situation.

You cannot change your ethnic origin. I cannot change my ethnic origin. I'm actually a Russian, German – Jew. (I should hate myself). But, I cannot change that. I like Mexican food and it just so happens, my son-in-law, Santiago was born in Mexico and came to America and became a citizen. Now, I could eat at a Mexican restaurant and eat hot sauce all day long but, at the end of the day, I am not a Mexican. I'm still a Russian, German – Jew. That is something I cannot change. So again don't waste your time on things you can't change.

It may take faith to change what you can. If you want something you never had, you may have to do something you've never done. Real faith is not based on theology or doctrine or a denominational creed. To stand the test of life in this pressure-cooker world, we need faith based on the impregnable, the infallible that can't, under any circumstance, be shaken. That is the Word of God, the Bible. God can go no farther than you believe Him to go. Your faith in God based on His word will help you succeed.

In my early years in ministry, my cash flow was tight. We prayed constantly for money to meet our needs so we could maintain our visitation program around Hazard Kentucky. One day I was left with one dollar to purchase gas. During my prayer time, I told the Lord, "I'm doing this for you and your people. Here I am without gas again, and my wife and I need to get to the service tonight. All I have is one dollar to last until my next miracle."

"What can I do for you?" the attendant asked as Barb and I pulled up to the pump of the local gas station. With as much pride as if I were getting a fill up, I said, "Give me a dollar's worth." Gas was about 25 cents per gallon.

After a few minutes passed, Barb asked, "Isn't he taking a long time just to put in a dollar's worth?" Turning to look out the window to where the attendant was pumping gas, I saw him shaking his head and mumbling, "Man, it's taking a long time for this gas to go in."

Looking at my gas gauge, I saw the needle moving toward "Full." "I hope he remembers that I told him just one dollar's worth," I said to Barb.

I yelled back, "Hey, I just want a dollar's worth!" "Yeah, I know," he replied. He pointed to the pump gauge, which registered .25 cents. "Something's wrong. This stuff is really going slow!"

Finally, he put away the hose and came to collect my dollar. When I drove away, my tank was full.

Another time the car was broke down. I could not fix it and after working on it, and trying for hours I was ready to give up. Disgusted, I looked at it and put down my tools. "Lord," I said, "I can't do anything else with this car. Maybe You can". The Bible says ask anything in Your name and you'll do it. Now I am asking.

Reaching out and putting one hand on the

engine and another in the air, I began praying out loud. I failed to hear the police officer pull up as I intently prayed, "Lord, please look down and fix the engine. I can't do it, and I need your help."

The policeman waited until I finished and the tapped me on the shoulder. When I turned to see who was there, he looked at me and said, "What in the world are you doing?" I said matter-of-factly, "I am praying for my car."

"Oh, what's wrong with it?" he asked. I shrugged and wiped the tears off my cheeks. "I don't know. That's why I'm praying for it!"

Pushing his helmet aside, he scratched his head. "You think it'll start now?" "Yes," I nodded. "God fixed it. I'll get in, and it will run" He laughed, "Before you get too excited, you'd better get in and try it. If it doesn't work, I'll call somebody." "Don't worry," I replied as I cleaned up my hands and slammed the hood down. "When I pray, it works!"

As I got into the car, the devil told me, "You're making a big fool of yourself! You'll never win that man to God. This is not going to be a testimony. He'll laugh at you." Refusing to let those words sink into my brain, I turned the key and the engine started immediately. I looked up into the face of the policeman as if God fixed cars every day! His face turned pale. "Man, I've seen everything!"

I told him that this was just the beginning of what God could do. After I told him about Jesus, he drove off on his motorcycle, a different man. God comes through when you trust Him.

But there are things that you can change. Sometimes if you change how you think about things, many times what you think about will even change. Some negative people like to keep records of other's wrongs. They like to discuss it, over and over. It is important that we think right and that we believe God and that we trust God. We need to show love too. It is because God has got this *Master Plan* for you.

> "Love is patient, love is kind. It does not envy, it does not boast, it is not proud. It does not dishonor others, it is not self-seeking, it is not easily angered, it keeps no record of wrongs. Love does not delight in evil but rejoices with the truth. It always protects, always trusts, always hopes, always perseveres. Love never fails....."
> 1st Corinthians 13:4-8 (NIV)

When I read Jeremiah it is so exciting.

The past we cannot do anything about whether it is good or bad. The past and the future do not even exist, it is now that exists! You can do something about the future if you make the right choices. What happens right now is so important. I believe and trust God in this hour. I believe that there are some great things that will happen in the future. I am believing for that. I am trusting God because I know that God will answer prayer because He has this *Master Plan* for me. You know, I really want to be a person that enjoys God and bears good fruit. Invitations to come and speak come to us all the time from some of the greatest churches in the world. I want to continue to bless churches, pastors and people, like I've done for over 60 years.

> Before I formed thee in the belly I knew thee; and before thou camest forth out of the womb I sanctified thee, and I ordained thee a prophet unto the nations.
> Jeremiah 1:5

God never calls a person to do something without giving them the necessary ability, the talent, the wisdom, the finances or whatever it takes to accomplish the task. Fit into what God has planned for you.

> *Be known for the fruit you bear,*
> *and not the fertilizer you are spreading.*

Remember you don't decide your future. You decide your habits and your habits decide your future. Change your habits, see if they are right, if they are lined up to the Bible. If not, get them changed. Your future depends on it.

In Luke 5, Jesus wanted to change Peter from being a failure to becoming a success. Peter said, "I've fished all night and caught nothing". Notice Jesus never mentioned his excuses. When you think you have exhausted all possibilities, you haven't. If your mind disbelieves something, it will attract reasons to support your disbeliefs. Jesus told Peter, the professional fisherman, how to fish, what to do, when to do it and where to do it. Peter obeyed and changed what he could. He fished in the day time, which they don't do. He fished in the deep water where there are no fish (they are in the 10-20 foot area where they feed). Guess what happened. He caught a boat load of fish. He also, called his friends and they caught a boatload of fish, too. Not only was he successful, he helped his friends become successful too. Obedience brought them success. Jesus was actually saying, you do what I am asking you to do and...
I will put fish where there are no fish.
I can give you a job when there are no jobs.
I can heal your body when there is no hope.
I can bless your business when others may fail.
I have a *Master Plan*.

1. **Change is Inevitable and Embracing Change Will Help You Grow**

    Because we dislike change, we sometimes go through life without ever living up to our full potential in God's plan. Change is an inevitable part of life and no matter how happy we are with how things are currently, life will always change.

    "The only thing constant is change." We know this and we understand that our environment can't stay the same forever. Embracing change is vital to growth.

2. **Analyze your Life and Find the Negative**

    Sometimes we change because we are attempting to rid negative habits or people from our lives. The sooner you become open to accepting change in your life, the better off you will be. Be constant in the way you analyze your life. What are the positives and more importantly, what are the negatives? The key to finding answers is that we focus on getting rid of the negative and building the positive side.

3. **Make Change While You Can, Before Change Makes You**

    It is better to initiate changes ourselves using free will than to let our life progress down a negative path until change affects us in a dramatic way.

Your attitude toward life is affected by your ability to embrace change. If change happens to you, rather than you influencing that change, you are much more likely to feel like you are being dragged through life. Embrace change with a calm and relaxed mind. Know where you are going and what you are setting out to accomplish. The clearer you picture these changes, the more motivated you will be.

4. **Everyone has Doubt, Fear and Uncertainty**

Everyone has fears that stop us from doing some things. Doubt and uncertainty are normal and you may never overcome it. However, what you can do is learn to embrace it. There may never be a time when you are completely absent of these thoughts and emotions; you will just learn to act anyway, regardless of whether they are there.

5. **Self Loathing is Counterproductive to Embracing Change**

Feeling sorry for yourself will always lead you down a negative path. It is counterproductive to God's plan for you. Never blame your surroundings for misfortune. Stay focused and set your sights high as you strive to achieve God's plan for you. As you stay focused, you will learn that embracing change becomes easier and easier. The overall message is that, wherever you are in life, value the journey. It takes time to accomplish anything worth achieving and we have to remember that it is a miracle that God has a plan for us and every step toward it must be appreciated.

It is important that we live the way that God wants us to live. Trust that He is going to help us to live like we are supposed to, as He is there to help us through every difficult situation. He wants to help us to get us through every negative situation that life throws at us. When negative things happen, say, "God will help me through this, because He has a *Master Plan* for me". I am a winner. I will be victorious. The *Master Plan* for my life will be totally successful.

I need to change...

1. _____

2. _____

3. _____

4. _____

Chapter 5
Be Positive In a
Negative World

We need to be positive with our thoughts and our words. How we think is important. What we say is important.

> Thou art snared with the words of thy mouth, thou art taken with the words of thy mouth.
> Proverbs 6:2

There are a lot of people that talk negative all the time. People often become what they think and say. We live in a troubled world. Gone are the dreams of many. Get a sure deal, a quick win, forget discernment, compassion, wisdom, excellence, empowerment, and role models. Do to them before they do to you. This is what many are saying or acting like. We should be inspired to be a role model to motivate others to do their best. If we are going to succeed and do great things, we may need to be different than others who try to steal our mantles and our dreams. They stand for nothing that is positive.

There are things that I do not like. I do not like mushrooms, I do not like cats and, I do not like opera music. We all have certain things that we do not like.

One thing that bothers me more than anything and I mention it all the time. I do not like to use negative words. I do not like negative thoughts or how negative people live. I do not even like negative songs. I turned the radio on one day and a guy was singing, "You picked a fine time to leave me, Lucille." What is that about? On another station, another guy was singing, "I was born with nothing, and I have most of it left." How negative is that? I like to hear positive songs about God being a miracle working God. That He can do the impossible and that He can answer prayer. I believe that is the way we must live. Our thinking has got to be right. This will help us get through the negative things.

If your thinking is wrong, your words will be wrong. If your words are wrong, your thinking is wrong. You have to change what you say and what you think. In a negative world, struggling for light, leadership, positive roles, and hope. We have to be the light they see during the storms. Don't be afraid to make a difference, inspire others to change, rebuking fear. Demand excellence. Some say, "Don't rock the boat". I say "Rock It!" Change negative ideas to positive ideas.

Be honest, demand excellence, demand courage and respect. Show kindness and seek wisdom of yourself. Know that God will see you through because He's got this *Master Plan* going for your life. Don't mess it up!

Again I say, nobody in life can make you a failure without your consent. You do not have to be a failure. God created us in His image. We have the DNA of God. Our God is a positive God. If our God is a positive God, then when He created you in His image, He created you as positive individual. If you have gotten negative, then you have gotten that way on your own. He created you in His image (positive) with His DNA. Remember this! Don't limit God!

Yea, they turned back and tempted God, and limited the Holy One of Israel.
　　　　　　　Psalms 78:41

Don't sabotage your freedom and success. You can if you allow it to. Don't let your fears and being negative grow into a tidal wave of worries that will wash away any hope of a dream. Don't stand in your own way by being negative. Your mind that wants to be positive will always be poisoned by negativity and doubt. Doubt is not just what we fail to do, it is who we fail to become. When thoughts of doubt turn into negative talking like:

What if:
    it won't work?
    I'm not a good enough person?
    I'm not strong enough?
    people will criticize me?
    people will use me?
    I fail?
    they laugh at me?

Faith in God will help the *Master Plan* to work for you. You choose to believe you can be successful at what ever you attempt, even in the face of odds that might be against you. When the odds are against you, God is against the odds. You will endure whatever situations you face, suffering, hardships, loss, etc. If you live like this, with all the doubts, negativities, etc. will be on their deathbed. I have found that FAITH is my favorite weapon against all the "what ifs."

Don't over think it, over pray it!
Debra Homan

I meet negative people all the time, They are worried about everything. But 90% of what they are worried about never happens. There are a lot of people just worried and are negative on a daily basis. Listen to them talk. It's always negative about everything. The house, the car, the job, the money, the kids, the pain, the church, the pastor, the president, etc. You should always talk positive about your family, your church, your pastor, and yes, about your wife/husband.

One lady on the airplane sitting beside me was coughing, said, "I am trying to catch a cold." I said, "I hope you are successful." I never argue with them, if they want something, then let them have it. You get what you believe for.

One lady in California picked up one of my Holy Land brochures and said, "Oh! I would love to go with you to Israel, but I will never go". I took the brochure and put it back! (No sense in wasting them.)

I believe you get what you believe for. God is a miracle working God. If you keep thinking and saying you cannot do something, you will be incapable of achieving it. On the other hand, if you say you can do something, God will help you achieve it. He does want to help you because He has a *Master Plan* for your life. Don't delay moving forward in faith. Action is required for a miracle. I love people like the Olympian runner who tripped during a race, but got up and caught the others and wins the race. Action will override fear.

We need to close the doors of our lives to negatives, to greed, to impossibilities, to fear, to unforgiveness and frustration. If you want to, you are able to close the doors of your life to fear, anger, negatives, greed, envy, jealously, unforgiveness, and anything that is not positive. You have the ability to open the doors of your life to God, to the Holy Spirit, to faith, to possibilities, to answers, to miracles, and to what God can do for you. I say this over and over. I don't believe in luck, good or bad. I do believe in God's divine blessings. I have said it many times that if corporations were run by luck they would fall apart. They don't put the names in a hat and draw them to see who has what position. They would not succeed if they ran a corporation on that basis.

I love to be around positive people. It encourages me. It lifts me up. That's better than having someone tearing you down. There are negative people that will just tear you down if you let them. If you spend your life looking for storms, you will never see the sunshine. Let the negative people talk negative, look for problems and storms. Some folks are just plain negative on everything. I called a friend on his birthday to bless him with a "happy birthday." His reaction was why did you wait until 5:00 pm to call me, he had to be negative. You should look for positive things and sunshine.

If you talk failure, it will hold you in bondage. If you talk sickness and bad health, you will feel worse. Doctors say they know many cases where people have imagined and said they were sick. What they confessed became true. If you always talk problems, you will never expect answers. If you talk poverty, you will stay broke. Why not start talking victory in every avenue of your life and see good stuff start to happen for you and to you. All great people in history fought their way out of the dark, out of fear, out of not knowing what to do and overcame all the difficulties that they faced to have a miracle. Yes, they probably were just like many of us, worried and scared at times, but they pushed forward in faith. They refused to give up. They stayed positive in the midst of defeat and became a winner.

> "Now unto him that is able to do exceeding abundantly above all that we ask or think, according to the power that worketh in us".
> Ephesians 3:20

God has a *Master Plan* for you. You will never receive more than you expect. Remember you were born with the positive DNA of God. You are a winner, you can jump hurdles, with God's help you can make things happen, you can achieve impossible goals. You are special, you are great, you are unique, you are the best, you are chosen and you are a wonderful creation of God. God does not make junk. He made you with His DNA. Live on the side of victory, on the answer side, on the positive side,

> *There is a miracle in motion for everybody.*
> *Don Lyon*

God created you to be a success. God created you to be a winner. God created you to rise above circumstances and believe that miracles will happen in your life. So know, if you talk failure, it is going to hold you in bondage. If you talk sickness, you will not feel good. If you talk fear, it can scare you. There are all kinds of things that can tear you down. Refuse to let your tongue talk negative. The main objective of satan is to deceive you. It is his job. He will come as an angel of light, but he is a liar, he deceives, he contradicts God's Word.

I love the story of a guy who one night walked into a cemetery and he fell into an open grave. He jumped and he jumped, but he just could not get out. So, he thought, "Well I will just sit here until morning and then someone would be able to help get me out." While he was sitting in the dark corner of the grave, another guy came through the cemetery and fell into the other end of the grave. He jumped and jumped and he could not get out either. The first guy said, "Bet you cannot make it out." And then, out he went. So, fear causes some things to happen. Let fear work for you not against you. Sometimes great things can happen with a little recklessness.

Again, I say in some way if you talk fear, it will hold you in bondage and defeat you. You talk poverty, you will stay broke, not having the answers you need.   You need a mindset for success. Your dreams can have more power than the circumstances and odds that are against you. What matters to some people is surviving in life not shaping it.

I met a guy on a plane. I said, "What do you do for a living?" He said, "I am a broker" I said, "You ever thought of being richer?" He never thought of that. That is the way it is, but God is trying to help us flow into the *Master Plan* he has for us.

There will always be people that will tear you down, try to steal your vision and dreams, even poison your mind and paralyze your thinking. They will try to defeat your blessings, and kill your dreams. In other words, they will try to highjack your future. Dexter Yeager wrote that great book about 40 years ago entitled *Don't Let Anybody Steal Your Dreams*. In the book Dexter said "You didn't ask to be here. God put you here so you must believe that He had a purpose for you".

There are some that actually believe they are right on everything all the time, on any subject. According to them, you are wrong and know nothing. They are always trying to prove they are right and you are wrong. They know everything about everything. They are, what I call, soul termites and sow seeds of destruction. Don't cave in to these people.

I call them uninformed experts in one of my books, *Answers to Questions You Always Wanted to Ask*. It talks about these negative people. They read books, know theories, but actually have no practical experience. They are not good working with family or people. Many times when they are present there is some kind of turmoil or trouble. Most uninformed experts know especially the negative aspects of any situation. People who are pessimists breed discouragement, they lack confidence and breed gloom. They are always quick to blame others for their problems, and most of the time can't see their own faults. Some, being miserable, seem to be happiest when they have made everyone around them as miserable as they are.

They have a need to control things. They are so insecure they can't admit to not knowing everything. They many times think management is wrong (unless they are management). They have no big vision for themselves. They don't even go after their dreams, because they have all the answers why it won't work, They find and know reasons why they can't achieve their dreams, no matter how many others have achieved theirs. Their life is a life filled with knowing everything about everything and doing nothing. They are immature. I feel so sorry for them.

> *Decide what you want in life,*
> *Then make it happen.*

We have been taking people on trips to Israel for over half our lives. Early on, through some trial and error, we learned how to conduct a deluxe tour with no gimmicks, no cutting corners to just save dollars. We wanted everything included with no extra charges or surprises in costs they didn't know in advance. Always rushing, trying to see everything but not remembering anything they saw. You usually get what you pay for. We have helped other pastors put tours together, and it is a passion that we love. Some pastors take tours to Israel, so when I am in their church I promote their tours. God always fills mine.

> Those things, which ye have both learned, and received, and heard, and seen in me, do: and the God of peace shall be with you.
> Philippians 4:9

Many people think they are experts in everything, but we can learn a lot from the people who have real knowledge.

Don't magnify your problems or situations. I love the story of Susan Butcher in Alaska. She raced dog sleds over 100,000 miles, on frozen rivers and snow. She received 4 awards for courage and 9 awards for speed. On a race from Nome to Anchorage, about 1100 miles, she was tired, wet, cold and exhausted. Even her dogs were tired and slowed down. With only about 30 some miles left she got off the sled and encouraged the dogs and finally fell over the finish line as she won. She said, "I knew I could do it". I love people like this.

> *JUST DO IT!*

We need to be positive in everything we do. God will outlast your problems. People who move the world are people that don't let the world move them. If you don't take action to move towards success in your life, you will always stay where you are. You'll not be successful or happy. We know actions allow us to connect, to create, to grow and even to rise above ourselves. All we want in life is to feel and experience satisfaction, success, love, joy, etc. It can only happen if there is some action. No one will grant you permission to have action in your life!

God has a *Master Plan* for our life so live positively, expecting good things to happen. Fear is the opposite of faith. Fear will rid you of your freedom. Some never have the life they really want. Some don't even chase their dreams because of the fear of failing. Declaring we will master our fear is the first step to faith and freedom. Remember, with God's *Master Plan*, you are too blessed to be stressed.

People will say:
- Be very careful, you never know what can go wrong.
- You really can't accomplish what you think you can.
- Some can do it but it is not you.
- Don't you worry about what can go wrong?
- Your goals will destroy you.

> Now faith is the substance of things hoped for, the evidence of things not seen.
> Hebrew 11:1

We must first believe that God exists and that He is a rewarder of those who seek Him. God is a God of success, our source. He made only one of you. Now satan is a deceiver, a devourer, a destroyer and a thief. Everything that satan has is stolen. He is negative and has a plan for your life that leads to ruin and destruction. He wants to totally wreck your future and mess up the *Master Plan* God has for you. Don't allow this to happen. God gave you the power to be a winner. Remember that a higher power (God) gave you the ability to win. Don't listen to anything negative.

Negative things I need to change...

1._____

2._____

3._____

4._____

Chapter 6
Raise The Level of Your Faith and Expectations

The sixth point is we have to raise the level of our faith and expectations. What is it you are expecting God to do for you? We are going to talk about some things that God gave me.

There are many bridges in your life. Everybody goes over bridges. You have to know which bridge to go over and which bridge to burn. God has a bridge leading from yesterday to tomorrow. A bridge from failure to success. He lets us hold onto wonderful, happy and great moments but leave behind old regrets. His bridge is for us to have joy, peace, happiness, and hope for the future. Have you ever noticed that life tends to respond to your outlook? Things usually go badly when you expect them to. You can't finish in faith until you get started in faith. You need to understand motivation. The word motive means "reason for action". Are you clear on reason? If so, you have a higher level of motivation and expectations. Do you expect a better way to succeed? A better home? A better body? A better marriage? A better life in general? Some people simply lack expectations. Some want to start their own business but never quit their job because they don't have higher expectations.

God wants you to raise the level of your faith and expectations. You never receive more than you expect. God wants to help you! Believe that God is on your side, He is not trying to kill you. He is trying to keep you alive; He is trying to help you. So use your faith. Many successful people in the world started with nothing. But they started anyway. Some always take more than they give. Others are givers and seem to always have more to give.

I married a policeman's daughter and I try to have answers in all situations. One time I got stopped and the policeman said, "I have been waiting for you." I said, "I got here as quick as I could!" It did not work! I expected a ticket and got one.

A man stopped at a motel during a bad rainstorm. He said, "I know the sign says, "No Vacancy". But I need a room. My wife is expecting and not feeling well. Is there any possible way that you have a room?" She said, "We have no rooms, we are completely sold out." He said, "If the President of the United States came here, would you have a room for him?" She said, "Well yes!" He said, "Well, he is not coming so I will take his room." I love people like that. That is believing for the impossible. If you want something you never had, you might have to do something you've never done.

Everyone is either on the building crew or wrecking crew. If you're on the building crew, you give, you sacrifice, you help, you bless, you go, etc. If you're on the wrecking crew you criticize, you grumble, you complain, you tear down, etc. Raise the level of your expectations. Live your life on the building crew side. When negative people try to tear you down, etc. raise the level of your expectations. I talk a lot about ignoring the dedicated agitators. Those who advance, move forward, accomplish goals, view it as positive. Negative people will even view advancing that the final outcome will be a negative. Some actually believe that the love of success or even money will bear better fruit. Some simpleminded people hate and don't trust because in order for someone to win, someone must lose. They blame others for successes. They must have lied, cheated etc. They say they couldn't have been honest and have success. They are on the wrecking crew.

I am a Christian! I serve a great God! I believe in miracles! I believe in the impossible becoming possible. Even in the secular world, business people have raised the level of their expectations and succeed greatly.

Frank W. Gunsaulus was just a regular Chicago minister. He wanted to help young people who had no funds to go to college. In 1890 he ran a newspaper ad stating that he would preach on "What I would do if I had one million dollars". His small church was packed. Philip Danforth Armour, owner and president of Armuor meat packing company, donated the million dollars to the minister so he could start Armour Institute of Technology (now Illinois Institute of Technology) which has become a great center of learning.

Henry Kaiser was asked by our government to build ships, but he built cars. He built a "Kaiser" and a "Frazer." And then, believe it or not, he built a Kaiser Frazer. Then he built a car I believe he named after his son called "Henry J." What does Henry Kaiser know about building ships? He never even built a canoe. But, he told our government, "I can do it!" They gave him the job, he signed the contract, and he put people around him that knew how to do it and he became a success. He built some of the greatest ships ever. So you see, he raised the level of his expectations. I admire people like that.

> For you are my rock and my fortress; and for your name's sake you lead me and guide me.
> Psalm 31:3

When I read this verse about God's *Master Plan* in our life, I know that God wants us to create the type of belief in our life that a miracle is in motion for us. Could you use a miracle in your life? Your part is to believe God. He has got this *Master Plan* all laid out for your life, for us to trust Him and for us to believe Him. Never be blinded by situations or discouraged by negative people.

When God made you, as I mentioned, He made you great, He made you wonderful, and He made you unique. He may have made you different, but He made you in His image. There is not another person in the world that has your finger prints. Isn't that wonderful! Everybody is made this way. God does not make junk! He made you! We have got something to be happy and excited about.

I get up every day and thank God for my family. At Thanksgiving, I thank God for my family, my blessings, and continue this daily. At Christmas, I praise God that Jesus was born. I continue to praise God daily for this. And at Easter I celebrate that we serve a risen Savior. This too I continue daily. Make your day count. Be thankful for every sunrise, for someday it will be your last one. Then at the end of each day count your blessings as the sun sets.

One lady on our Israel tour looked inside the tomb and said, "There is nothing in there!" Our guide said, that is why what we have is different than the Muslims and the Hindus and the Buddhist. We serve a risen Savior. We have something to be excited about. We have got something to be thrilled about. Raise the level of your expectations and know that God will help you.

When they asked Thomas Edison, "How does it feel to fail over 700 times?" You know what he said? He said, "I did not fail. I just found 700 ways that won't work. But I will find the way that does work". He had over 10,000 so called failures. We know the name Thomas Edison, because he raised the level of his expectations. He believed!

Walt Disney's brother said to him "You are

crazy to build a Disneyland! The kids have no money; the parents are not going to give them the money. Listen, you are going to lose your shirt." But, let me ask you one question, what was the name of Walt Disney's brother? His name will never really be remembered, like Walt. It is Walt Disney we will always remember. He raised the level of his expectations.

Colonel Sanders was broke at sixty-five years old. He was so broke that he slept in his car, he could not afford a motel. But, he said I will put Kentucky Fried Chicken all over the world, and he did just that. Because he raised the level of his thinking and his expectations.

Think of Ray Kroc, at 52 years old, that founded McDonald's. He looked for a name that would work. He raised the level of his expectations. He found the Mac and Dick McDonald brothers, who had McDonald hamburgers. He bought their name and said, "McDonald's that will work!" Ray Kroc probably thought that "Kroc burgers" would never sell. So, he raised the level of expectations and said, "McDonald's will sell! It became a household name." Think about successful people who achieved great things. They were not negative, angry, bitter, unhappy people. Ray Kroc opened the 1st McDonalds with the first day revenue of $366.12 and today it is well known with more than 30,000 McDonalds in over 100 countries serving millions of people daily, making billions of dollars.

You see, if the secular world can raise the level of their expectations, if you are a Christian you can do this also. We can believe that God will see us through. I am raising the level of my expectations all the time. I believe that every year is going to be the greatest year. I believe that it is going to be good spiritually, physically, financially, and emotionally in every way. I believe God is helping us because He has a *Master Plan* that is going to work. There are many stories of men and woman who started with nothing and climbed over every hurdle, jumped every negativity, became masters at doing whatever and crossed impossible mountains in spite of obstacles against them to win the battles. God says, "So, I've got this *Master Plan* for your life." This should excite you!

> Trust
> Fills in the blanks
> until the blanks can be filled in.
> Dana Gammill

Give God a chance in your life. Let God help you. If you do not know Christ, turn your life over to Him for the *Master Plan* to work for you.

I hate to see good people end up spending eternity in Hell. I think that it is important that people find the Lord. People that give God a chance in their life, they raise the level of their expectations. You might be saying, "I have not been happy this year. Things have not been going good for me, but I am going to give God a chance in my life and I know God will see me through, and I know God will give me a miracle." "I need a change in my life. I know that God has a *Master Plan* for me and I have messed it up, but I want God to help me. I want God to straighten it out for me. I want things to be better. In the future, I want God to see me through." I believe that God will touch my life and that God will help me, if I just give Him a chance and I am going to do it. God has a *Master Plan* for my life. That is a great start.

You say, so many bad things have happened. God can turn that around and make good things happen to you. Give God a chance right now, to work that *Master Plan*. One of the best ways to get the *Master Plan* to work is to give your life to Christ. Put Him first in your life. You may not be a bad person, you just need Jesus to turn things around, as you give Him your life. Let's believe that God will turn things around. Say, "I am making a change. I will jump over negative hurdles. I will, with God's help, achieve my goals, I am a winner, and with God's help, I will win every battle. God is going to do good things in my life and this is just the start." Don't be like the man building his house and realizes it may house the devil someday, so he quit and put away his tools.

If you get involved with God, God will get involved with you. If you get involved with God's dream, God will get involved with your dreams. God does not supply according to our needs, our brains, our IQ, our job, our education, our talent or our ability. Put your faith in Him and watch the *Master Plan* start to work.

As you live for Him, start thanking God daily that your faith in Him will help you in every avenue of your life. The *Master Plan* God has for you is just around the corner. You are on the brink of great things. You are on the brink of a miracle.

To raise my level of faith and expectation I need to change...

1._____

2._____

3._____

4._____

The Master Plan God Has for You

As with everyone, God has a *Master Plan* for us. Since we are all different, everyone's *Master Plan* is slightly different. It doesn't make any difference what nationality you are, the color of your skin, what language you speak or where you live.

> "But my God shall supply all your need according to his riches in glory by Christ Jesus.
> Philippians 4:19

1. Put God First In Your Life.

This means surrendering your will to God's. Many times when we say we are seeking God's plan, what we are really wanting to say to God is this: "OK, God, here's what I'm planning to do. Now I need you to rubber stamp this, all right?" I must tell you that this is not really effective in finding His true plan. Before God will begin to reveal His plan to you, you must be committed to doing whatever it is that He desires for you to do. God is more likely to be slow to show you His plan if He knows you won't do the plan anyway.

> [1] I beseech you therefore, brethren, by the mercies of God, that ye present your bodies a living sacrifice, holy, acceptable unto God, which is your reasonable service. [2] And be not conformed to this world: but be ye transformed by the renewing of your mind, that ye may prove what is that good, and acceptable, and perfect, will of God.
>
> Romans 12:1-2

> God will always prepare you
> for where He is going to take you.
>
> Jerry Beebe

This is number one (1). Put God first in your life. It has worked for me and millions of other people all over the world.

> "But seek ye first the kingdom of God, and his righteousness; and all these things shall be added unto you".
> Matthew 6:33

2. *Ask God To Help You.*

Asking God to help you scripturally. He will give you power and authority.

> "Ask of me, and I shall give thee the heathen for thine inheritance, and the uttermost parts of the earth for thy possession".
> Psalm 2:8
>
> "Then he called his twelve disciples together, and gave them power and authority over all devils, and to cure diseases".
> Luke 9:1

3. Obey what you already know to be God's Will.

Many people seem to want to know what God's plan is for their lives, but they overlook the fact that 99% of His will is already written carefully through His Word. God is very clear about many, many aspects of His will. For instance, it is clearly His plan that we abstain from sexual immorality.

> For this is the will of God, even your sanctification, that ye should abstain from fornication:
> 1 Thessalonians 4:3

If we do not obey the things that God has already shown us to be His will, why would we think He would reveal any further information regarding His plan for our lives? Obedience is an important step.

4. Sow a big harvest.

Be a big giver. You will harvest a large harvest.

> "But this I say, He which soweth sparingly shall reap also sparingly; and he which soweth bountifully shall reap also bountifully."
> 2 Corinthians 9:6

5. Thank God for good health and freedom from disease and pain.

It is all yours for thanking God.

> "Then shall thy light break forth as the morning, and thine health shall spring forth speedily: and thy righteousness shall go before thee; the glory of the LORD shall be thy reward".
> Isaiah 58:8

6. Thank God (in advance) for the miracles you need.

Read Psalm 23. David knew how to pray. When the odds are against you, God is against the odds.

¹ The LORD is my shepherd; I shall not want. ² He maketh me to lie down in green pastures: he leadeth me beside the still waters. ³ He restoreth my soul: he leadeth me in the paths of righteousness for his name's sake. ⁴ Yea, though I walk through the valley of the shadow of death, I will fear no evil: for thou art with me; thy rod and thy staff they comfort me. ⁵ Thou preparest a table before me in the presence of mine enemies: thou anointest my head with oil; my cup runneth over. ⁶ Surely goodness and mercy shall follow me all the days of my life: and I will dwell in the house of the LORD for ever.

Psalm 23

I will do the following...

1. From today forward I will put God first.
2. I will ask God for help in all things.
3. I will be obedient to God and listen to His will.
4. I will sow a big harvest.
5. I will be thankful for all He has done for me.
6. I will thank God in advance for all He will do in the future.

Ken Gaub travels all over the world
and may be coming to your area.
If you would like to receive his monthly e-letter,
please send your e-mail address to:
becki@kengaub.com.

If you would like to write to the author,
order his other books, DVD etc.
or schedule him to speak,
contact him through:

Ken Gaub World Wide Ministries
P.O. Box 1
Yakima, WA 98907 U.S.A.
Phone: (509) 575-1965
Fax: (509) 575-4732
email: becki@kengaub.com
website: www.kengaub.com

Made in United States
Orlando, FL
07 April 2024